Reversing Willie Lynch's Slave Making Method

Publish Work

Ten-Part Book to Maximizing Your Potential
Life Poems
Three-Part Process to Breaking the Recidivism Cycle
Redeeming the Time
Young, Gifted and Black
50 Most Positive Things I Know About African Americans
Trust God
Stopping the Tragic Lost of Life Caused by Purposeless Living
Pandemic Survival Manual
Let Them Eat Cake
Don't Judge, Hug
The Wheel Life Story of Dionte Christian
God Is Bigger
Treating Our Common Wound
Parenting Tips for A New Age

Reversing Willie Lynch's Slave Making Method

Danny Ray Christian

To order additional copies of this book, contact:
Xlibris
844-714-8691
www.Xlibris.com
Orders@Xlibris.com
835776

All biographical profiles were taken from Wikipedia, the Free Encyclopedia.

Contents

Dedication

*This book is dedicated to all the martyrs who made
the ultimate sacrifice for the liberation of our people
from the various forms of enslavement we have
endured here in America for four-hundred years, and
those who have been cut down in their prime by the
perpetrators of black-on-black violence and police
brutality, who are martyrs in their own right.*

Thesis

"Is it possible for a race and community to be traumatized by a painful experience to the extent that it affects how their DNA responds to certain environmental stimuli, and is passed on to their offspring?" It is my belief that such a phenomenon is possible, and I will put forth evidence to prove it. My objective is to help African Americans who are living with the Post Trauma of Slavery (PTSD), to move beyond their trauma. Also, I want to supply information on how we can stop the transference of the trauma of slavery to future generations through our DNA.

Introduction

*The history and dynamics of PTSD and
transference of trauma through DNA.*

First and foremost it must be clarified 'What is trauma?' Webster Dictionary defines trauma as; Trauma is **an emotional response to a terrible event like an accident, rape or natural disaster**. Immediately after the event, shock and denial are typical. Longer term reactions include unpredictable emotions, flashbacks, strained relationships and even physical symptoms like headaches or nausea.

If I wanted to I could stop here and rest my case that not only were our ancestors traumatized by slavery but that we still continue to feel its effects on our lives, community, relationships and behavior. Trauma is not the terrible event or experience itself but our response to it. Trauma is deeply personal, meaning that it must be perceived as an intentional attack upon our general wellbeing.

Though the initial shock of terrible events wears off over time, the experience is never completely forgotten.

For example; Having once been bitten by a dog you are forever henceforth a little leary of dogs. Even if you are ever bitten by a dog again, you will always carry an image of the dog that bit you in your mind. In the same sense I believe slavery has caused African Americans to be apprenensive about letting their guards down around white people. We carry vivid memories of them repeatedly attacking us like vicious dogs and haunting us down with the same when we struck out for freedom (peacefully protesting the continuation of **Jim Crowism,** in Montgomery Alabama). Perhaps the unforeseen effect of the dog biting you is that it makes you become a little like it and start to attack anyone who gets close to you – that steps within your yard (space). The ever-increasing acts of black-on-black crime and violence gives credit to this analogy. "Once bitten twice smitten!"

What are the three types of trauma?

There are three main types of trauma: Acute, Chronic, or Complex

- Acute trauma results from a single incident.
- Chronic trauma is repeated and prolonged such as domestic violence or abuse.
- Complex trauma is exposure to varied and multiple traumatic events, often of an invasive, interpersonal nature.

"Guilty on all three counts!" Our ancestor's enslavement was (a) acute to the extent that it singularly sought to dehumanize them by calling them $3/5^{th}$ human and listing them as "chattel property" on census documents. It was (b) chronic via daily infliction of both physical abuse through forced labor in cotton fields from 'can't see in the morning until can't see at night' and repeated rape of the women and castration of the men. It was (c) complex to the degree that it dominated their whole existence, making them question their own self-worth, as evidenced by them affixing their identity and concept of self to that of the slave master. When he was sick, the house slave's response was to say, "is us sick, Master?"

Moving forward, we see that we are dealing with an 'acute, chronic and complex' trauma which will require acute, chronic and complex treatment in order for it to be effectively reversed (managed).

What is the DSM-5 definition of trauma?

The DSM-5 definition of trauma requires **"actual or threatened death, serious injury, or sexual violence"** [10] (p. 271). Stressful events not involving an immediate threat to life or physical injury such as psychosocial stressors [4] (e.g., divorce or job loss) are not considered trauma in this definition. Feb 13, 2017

The DSM-5 is the 'Diagnostic and Statistical Manual of Mental Disorders.' On this point we do not have to go all the way back to slavery to see that those in the African American community (inner-city) meet the DSM-5 critire for being declared trauma victims and therefore can be diagnosied as suffering from a mental disorder and in need of treatment for a legtimate mental disorder, due to our living under a state of sedge, where our lives are either threatened or snuffed out by the police as well as other Blacks, who have no respect for black life. For the most part though we meet the DSM-5 designation as being traumatized (mentally ill), we ourselves and the CDC, have ignored this fact, and failed to allocate the resources to help us manage and/or treat our mental disorder.

Just looking at the "actual or threatened death" part of the DSM-5 requirement for the diagnosis of trauma, it is apparent that African Americans more than any other segment of this society, encounters daily threats to their lives. Many of us live in actual war zones as rival gangs terrorize our children and neighborhoods with gun violence – fighting over drug turf. It is worth noting that trauma is described by the DSM-5 as a 'mental disorder' and not a mental sickness, the differentiation being that a 'disorder' is misfestated in erratic changes in behavior, where 'illnesses' take their greatest toll on the physical body. The symptoms of the disorder can be alleviated with a change in environment and the removal of the trauma causing agents (individuals), thus leading to the possibility of recovery or at least improvement.

Can trauma be cured?

Is There a Cure for PTSD? As with most mental illnesses, **no cure exists for PTSD**, but the symptoms can be effectively managed to restore the affected individual to normal functioning. The best hope for treating PTSD is a combination of medication and therapy. As a person diagnosed with a mental disorder, (Schizoaffective Disorder Bipolar Type.

Schizoaffective disorder is a combination of symptoms of schizophrenia and mood disorder, such as depression or bipolar disorder. Symptoms may occur at the same time or at different times. Cycles of severe symptoms are often followed by periods of improvement. Symptoms may include delusions, hallucinations, depressed episodes, and manic periods of high energy.

People with this disorder generally do best with a combination of medications and counseling.)

I can testify that a "well managed mental disorder is as good as a cured disorder." With this hope I am confident that we can get better, once we acknowledge first that our ancestors were traumatized by slavery and second that the trauma has been passed down through our genes until this day, so much so, that we fit the DSM-5 criteria for being mentally ill – need treatment for behavioral disorder brought on by 'acute, chronic and complex trauma' directed at us historically, systemically and daily in America via all its institutions and media channels.

I am not in agreement with the statement that there is, 'no cure exists for PTSD' or any other bonafide mental disorder. I believe every disease can be cured, understanding that the word "disease" taken apart simply means, 'dis-ease.' Having a disease means that a person or group is in a state of being dis-at-ease. When we put ourselves back at-ease, disease disappears. Meditation (prayer, focus on The Divine), the oldest and most effective form of medicine known to man, is the cure. In other words, when peace is restored to our mind; our bodies, souls, spirits, relationships and communities will feel and bear proof of our healing – restored sanity.

Since the beginning of time man's initial response to trauma has been to act out with violence, especially, toward those he perceived as being the cause or agent of the trauma.

Having all of the above as the premise for my argument, that not only did slavery traumatize our ancestors and the trauma has been passed down for generations through our DNA, but also that such trauma can be reversed and its transference stoped, I present to you the means whereby we can "Reverse the process, whereby our ancestors were traumatized for four-hundred years, to the point that we have inherited its effects through our DNA, ending the legacy of Willie Lynch."

Overview

The Science of Transgenerational Trauma

What are cells?

In biology, the smallest unit that can live on its own and that makes up all living organisms and the tissues of the body. A cell has three main parts: the cell membrane, the nucleus, and the cytoplasm. The cell membrane surrounds the cell and controls the substances that go into and out of the cell.

As living organisms, cells, like every other living organism, are influenced by its environment as well as the overall wellbeing of its host. Thus, it is a nobrainry, to figure out that trauma can be transferred from the original organism to all its offspring. This observation is the basis for my propossition that the trauma our ancestors experienced in slavery has in fact beenpassed on to every preceding generation of African Americans.

Our genes play an important role in our health, but so do our behaviors and environment, such as what we eat and how physically active we are. Epigenetics is the study of how our behaviors and environment can cause changes that affect the way our genes work. Unlike genetic changes, epigenetic changes are reversible and do not change our DNA sequence, but they can change how our body reads a DNA sequence. (CDC).

How is generational trauma passed?

Enslavement, genocide, domestic violence, sexual abuse, and extreme poverty are all common sources of trauma that lead to intergenerational trauma. A lack of therapy also worsens symptoms and can lead to transmission.

Before I proceed with my prescription for undoing what slavery did to us not only on a mental, physical and spiritual level, but also on a cellular level, I would like to point out a few sayings (Scriptures and Proverbs) that have supported the idea that trauma can be passed on through DNA for thousands of years.

I first take you to Lamentations 5:7 kjv, "In those days they shall say no more, '**The fathers** have **eaten** a sour **grape, and the children's teeth are set on edge.**'" Jeremiah 31:30, "But everyone shall die for his own iniquity: every man that **eateth** the sour **grape**, his **teeth** shall be **set** on **edge.**"

These two verses of Scripture from the Holy Bible make it obvious that people have known for thousands of years that whatever bitter experiences the father encountered, using the analogy of eating sour grapes, was passed down to his children, in the form of their being put on edge (acting out) for unknown reasons. Jeremiah follows this piece of evidence supporting inherited trauma by noting that there would come a time when the children will be free of their father's trauma. I feel that I need say no more about these two Scriptures and pieces of ancient wisdom concerning Post Traumatic Stress being passed down through DNA.

For my next piece of evidence, before I talk about how to reverse Willie Lynch's slave making method, I will provide a piece of folklore. There is an old saying, "The apple doesn't fall far from the tree." We have said this for years about our sons and daughters who have all our characteristics despite not being raised by us. So, once again there is proof that we have instinctively known for generations that trauma along with other characteristics can be passed to future generations through DNA. Thus, it would do us and our descendants a lot of good if we examined how we can stop the passing on of trauma through our DNA. I warn you that I am no geneticist or trauma expert, I am applying my God given common sense to the matter. I believe we must reverse the process of how we were traumatized by slavery, to get to the point of recalibrating our genetic blueprint from one enwrapped with trauma (weakness, dis-ease) to one enarmored with strength and harmony.

Step 1
Strict Discipline

Willie Lynch's first piece of advice to white slave owners who wanted to better control our ancestors was to enforce the strictest form of discipline on them possible. While discipline, most notably, self-discipline, is an inherently good trait to have, if it is forced on you, you can develop an innate hatred for it. In a roundabout way therefore when prisoners are released from prison or slaves emancipated from slavery, they want nothing more than to experience a life without restrictions and the freedom to roam. I believe that a general dislike for discipline was one of the negative effects of slavery that has been passed down through our genes, to the point that many of us either seek to avoid it or exercise it only under duress. In the prisoner's or slave's eyes the sign of a free man is being able to do what he wants while others do all the hard work. "It is the privilege of the master to sit on the porch or in the shade sipping a mint julep while the slaves work the fields in the hot sun."

If I fed you a diet of nothing but vegetables every day for years, though all you wanted is some fried chicken and chocolate cake, there is a good chance that you would grow to hate vegetables despite how healthy they are. Using the same method, hate which is a learned behavior, can be bred into you. So as far as Willie Lynch instructing white owners to enforce strict discipline on our ancestors, as a means of turning them into more compliant slaves, he essentially set the stage for them to hate discipline (getting up before dawn to work the fields until can't see at night). For this reason I believe that there are certain aspects of discipline that go unappreciated by individuals who have previously been forced to work hard for others' profit.

Keeping the focus on the transference of trauma through DNA to our offspring, I must provide more than theoretical evidence that African Americans have a disproportionate disdain for discipline (hard work).

Let me ask you, "Have there ever been times when you felt that you were working harder than others, while continuing to fall behind and be underpaid?" In the back of your mind did you not tell yourself, what is the use in you continuing to work hard with no apparent payoff? My empirical evidence for proving this part of my thesis is your own admission that you are less likely to stay on such a job that does not equally compensate you for the work you put into it. And if you have experienced the same discrimination at all your other jobs, you will inevitably develop a cavalier attitude toward the very thing you need to do in order to eventually out pace those who are trying to hold you back. Looking at the supposition that though strict discipline is an innately positive trait, we associate it with the trauma our ancestors experienced at the hands of whites, from the perspective of the aforementioned example, surely you can see how we have been made to 'hate that which is good for us.'

Forced compliance is always met with some resistance. Until this day there are whites in this society who still resist the demand for Reparations being paid to the descendants of African Americans, who were clearly deprived of pay for four-hundred years of hard labor. Even more relevant is the resistance millions of Americans have for the mandate of masks being worn to stop the spread of the COVID-19 virus, least of all mandated vaccinations. All this goes to show that the trauma of slavery, specifically, how it was maintained through the use of the whip, tarring and castration, to enforce strict discipline upon those held in slavery for generations. This happened to the point that now we have those among us who must reimagine how self-discipline along with consistency can in fact begin to loosen the shackles of slavery from our minds.

What is needed to reverse the effect of this part of Willie Lynch's slave making process and stop it from being transferred to the next generation? We must take ownership of the good that comes from having strict discipline. Now we can use it to build up ourselves and our community. We can work appreciation for discipline back into our genes by making a habit of putting

self-development before self-indulgence. I am confident that if we do this over a significant period, that it will become as natural for us as it is now for us to take every break, holiday and vacation that we can, whether we can afford it, are tired or have achieved parity or not.

Step 2
Sense of Inferiority

This portion of Willie Lynch's blueprint for making slaves was achieved with the oldest method of creating a sense of inferiority in a person or race, known to man. Basically, all an enslaver needs to do to make the people he wants to serve him without much resistance is convince his captives that he is God or at least the descendant of God, where they are lower creatures. To gain the power of God and the right of God to rule over the earth as well as every other race/group, all that is required is for you to first paint God in your image and then paint yourself in his image (**Michelangelo's Sistine Chapel portrait of God and all the Host of Heaven**). This fait can be said to have been effectively accomplished by white slave owners 'whitewashing of both the Bible and history, where everyone of any significance was declared to be of the white race.

What this did to alter our DNA and traumatize us, was to make our ancestors question not only their own beauty and history but also their relation to the Creator. This doubt instilled within their psyche; it was not too difficult to get them to comply with slave owners' commands. Once again drawing on the old saying, "The apple doesn't fall far from the tree," there is something about when a woman is pregnant and she is consumed with feelings of worthlessness, the baby within her stomach becomes lethargic. Every midwife knows that confident mothers give birth to vibrant babies.

This premise brings me to the point that certain traits can both be bred into and bred out of animals and as well as races, through selective breeding. This is done to domesticate wild animals every day. All white slave owners had to do in order to achieve the creation of a sense of inferiority as prescribed by Willie Lynch, in our ancestors, was to weed out the rebellious fieldhands through public execution, while promoting the more docile slaves to the Big House. Those who would not consent to being a slave for any reason or "living on their knees," died on their feet! For them there was no point in living if they could not live as men and women of dignity. **They clearly knew that only slaves birthed slaves.** So the goal of creating and transferring degenerate genes was succinctly accomplished in the very continuation of our lives under a system that did not allow for the existence of such warriors as Nat Turner and Denmark Vesey (Black insurrectionists).

A **god complex** is an unshakable belief characterized by consistently inflated feelings of personal ability, privilege, or infallibility. A person with a god complex may refuse to admit the possibility of their error or failure, even in the face of irrefutable evidence, intractable problems or difficult or impossible tasks. The person is also highly dogmatic in their views, meaning the person speaks of their personal opinions as though they were unquestionably correct.[1] Someone with a god complex may exhibit no regard for the conventions and demands of society, and may request special consideration or privileges.[1]

It is not far to accuse all white men of having a 'god complex,' no more than it would be to pose that every victim of trauma (enslavement, mentional, physical or emotional abuse) will develop an inferiority complex. But looking at his history in the Common Era and how murder and mayhamn has followed him everywhere he has gone, the white man clearly demonstrates many of the characteristics of one with a 'god complex.' The dropping of the atomic bomb on Hiroshima (August 6, 1945) and on Nagasaki (August 9, 1945) during World War II, as ordered by President Harry S. Truman, proves that one man and one nation under the delusion of a 'god complex' poses a threat to humanity's continual existence.

It is clearly a sign of mental disability and moral debauchery for a human to even imagine and want to create a weapon of mass destruction which can literally wipe all life from the face of the earth: least of all not only threaten to use it but actually drop it on not one but two cities filled with innocent men, women and children.

In the Art of War, the only way to defeat someone who is diabolical and merciless is to be even more diabolical and merciless. Contrayaly, the merciful humanity is used against him, in the sense that he can be counted on to not cross the line of what distinguishes him from 'the beast' (merciless). In other words, "He can't defeat his enemy because he won't become his enemy!" This moral restraint has brought great satisfaction to the hearts of conquers and perpetrators of genocide throughout history. You can tell me how you are morally superior to me all you want, as long as I am able to ride your back and play proxy to your God and manhood, as you do so. You will effectively have your 'Moral Pie' made of tears and pipe dreams, while I enjoy my 'Black Gold,' made of your sweat and blood. Thus, the good continues to die while the evil grows more vicious.

A man (race, nation or believer) with a 'god complex' is dangerous enough, but anyone who has a messiah complex or even worse a martyr complex, is infinitely more dangerous. People with a 'god complex' will sacrifice others to achieve their grandiose ideas and self-enthronement, but they are not too quick to sacrifice themselves. Isis fighters and members of the Taliban are willing to die by the hundreds because they believe that they will receive the reward of martyrdom for defending their religion, Islam. All of us possess all three complexes (god, messiah and martyr) to one degree or another. Some of us just display one complex more strongly than others; and that is what makes us a danger to others, when we either believe, "we are gods, messiahs or martyrs".

I make this note of the 'god complex' which I believe caused white slave owners, to attempt to create a sense of inferiority in African Americans they held in slavery, for the purpose of showing how every narcissist ultimately must have two things in order to maintain his/her sense of grandeur: 1. a mirror or other way to adore his own reflection, and 2. someone he can make himself superior to through belittlement and debasement. History is full of a litany of men and nations that have tried to cleanse the earth of those they deemed as "undesirables" and scourges, when they themselves were the scourges. I need not name, names, for their names and the atrocities they committed are well known. Suffice it to say, that this narcissism continues in the likelihood that the COVID-19 virus is indeed a man-made patheon created as a biological weapon of war.

So, "what is my recommendation for halting the transference of this traumatic remnant of slavery through our DNA to the next generation?" It is twofold, first we must once again know that we are as much 'The Sons and Daughters of God' as anyone else; secondly, we must live our lives at a level of excellence where there is no room to question whether we deem any race superior to us. Put in simple words, I believe we can cause a mutation in our DNA to the effect that we feed this generation the wholesome milk of unquestionable dignity and irrefutable integrity and undefeatable tensicity. This way we will assure that all Black children born, henceforth, will be as strong and courageous as those of our ancestors who refused to live as slaves.

The man who wakes up a slave and goes to bed a slave, loses the chance between sunrise and sunset to break the chains of slavery, and thus should expect to wakeup a worse slave tomrrow. And he deceives himself if he believes that his endurance of his enslavement makes him a better man. Every slave owner can happily live with such self-deception on the part of his slaves, while he knows the truth, that if they would be men, he would not be able to hold them in slavery beyond one day, minute or hour, definitely not for generations.

Step 3
Belief in Master's (Whites) Superior Power

"At what point did our ancestors intrinsically start to believe in the superiority of white's power, right to rule over them, or did they ever truly accept such?"

I am doubtful that our ancestors ever believed in white's superior power or superiority in a conceptual sense where they articulated it in the conversation with either themselves or one another. But it is obvious that they believed this about whites, to the extent that they lived their lives in accordance with their rules and objective of making them their slaves. If I were your boss at work, I would not need you to call me, Boss, and acknowledge me as being superior to you in any way, because your compliance with my authority would say it all, albeit, that you would do so for the sake of keeping your job. On the other hand, if I were a domineering boss, who constantly treated you like an inferior subject and talked to you in a demeaning manner every day, your tolerance of this type of treatment would ultimately cause some feelings of self-doubt and self-loathing to seep into your conscience.

It was not necessary for our ancestors to verbalize any feelings or belief in the superiority of whites. By them tolerating their dehumanizing daily torture they affirmed such through complacency. You and I can tell ourselves that, "We fear nor bow down to no man," as a means of looking confident, but if we nevertheless work the fields for four-hundred years without pay, we will prove that this bravo is just words.

For the time that we were literal slaves in the country, there was something else going on within our psyche and molecular development that was not perceivable on the surface of our character and daily behavior. We were effectively being amalgamated into a slave culture, which would always put us in a position of having to detangle ourselves, from a past that we have to defend with psychological triculation and mental aquabats. Meaning, that we had to try and make sense out of what we allowed white people to do to us for four-hundred years. In essence what was occurring beneath the surface of our psyche, our ancestors developed a subtle endearment for their slave masters. They experienced what has become known as the "Stockholm Syndrome."

I have no documented proof that any of our ancestors actually displayed evidence of having positive feelings towards those who held them in slavery, but it is alegded that certain of them did have such sentiments. It has been reported and portrayed in film that those known as 'house niggers' would say such things as, "Is us sick Master" as though they and their owners were one-and-the-same person. The house slaves were so grateful to their owners for taking them out of the fields, that they would not only cry when they died, but would also report any uprising planned by the "field niggers." This sense of endearment was so intense that if the house slave was told that they were going to be sold, they would pray and beg their owners to sell them to some more "Good White Folks." The implication was that even though they were not being emancipated that it was possible to be humanely held in subgegation to another man's will and abuse.

Yet I do not judge those of our ancestors who fell in love with their owners, because it is just a part of all our nature as humans, to grab for and hold on to the least show and sign of affection from those who abuse us. Just as every dog wants its own bone, every man, woman and child wants to be loved, even if that love has to come from psychopaths and sadistic abusers. For the sake of our sanity sometimes we have to, when in unfavorable circumstances or abusive relationships, dress demons in angels' gowns. Our mind does this as a means of maintaining its continuity. The indication of the reason captives become friends with their captors is because the only way overwhelming suffering and incomprehensible cruelty can be survived by humans, is by us reimagining our abusers as

Saints and seeing ourselves as Sinners in need of purging and deserving of punishment.

How this aspect of the trauma of our ancestors' enslavement affected their DNA, occurred by way of them training their mind to minimize and conceptualize immeasurable pain and despair, as not being 'that bad.' Our genetic code is as much written by the regeneration of our healthy cells as by the stressors we expose our body to. Humanity has only been able to survive the traumatic experiences of our lives and history through the process of our genes innately knowing how to adapt whatever is required to keep us alive. In other words, we learn to either "fight or flight" with our entire being; we fight with our cellular metabolism as well as with our hands and body.

Battles are not always won by the army with the superior weapons but by the one which has the most confidence in its weapons and themselves. I use the well-known example of David defeating Goliath with a slingshot. This principle was obviously known to Willie Lynch, which is why he instructed white slave owners to do their best to make their slaves believe that they had the 'Might of Right' (otherwise known as White) on their side. This traumatic deception was achieved by whites drilling in our heads that everything white, starting with their skin, was pure and thereby more powerful, whereas everything black, starting with our skin, was evil, and therefore weak and inferior. Initially when they first came to Africa, we thought they were ghosts, and that they had risen from the dead. They took advantage of this fear by terrorizing us with burning crosses while wearing white KKK outfits.

The bottom line is that over a period of four-hundred years of being told that "might (white) determines right" we inevitably came to question the innate strength and power of our own skin and culture. As a result of us being whipped or hung when we dared to rebel against the supposition that we could not be men, because only people with the power of the whip, gun and Bible were ordained to rule as real men, we were traumatized by the very skin we felt forced to live in. (Frantz Fanon, "Black Skin, White Mask" 1952). We proved this manifestation of trauma by bleaching our skin and straightening our hair the first chance we got, so much so that the first Black millionaire Madame C.J. Walker made millions from the invention and use of the straightening comb and other black hair products.

Reversing this traumatic remnant from slavery may prove the most difficult because we still want to look good, and that basically means, we want our hair straight and or skin bleached (though to a lesser degree than we did in the past). Now the youth wear naturals more than processes. I will admit that since I am Old School, when I see them with what I would call "unkempt" hair, that they need "to comb their hair." I even feel self-conscious when my own beard and hair gets out of hand, and I tell myself that I need a shave and haircut. This shows that I have been conditioned to think of straight hair as being "good hair" and a "clean face" as being more appealing.

Today's black youth have traded straight hair and bleached skin for tatted up bodies, draped in expensive clothing, which exceeds their income. But for those of us who want to start a new trend with our children we must stop acting like our skin and hair is a curse and start to live in it as proudly as we would in a million dollar mansion. Trying to become comfortable in our own skin again while at the same time covering it with tattoos and hiding behind Name Brands, is equivalent to a smoker saying he wants to stop smoking while lighting up a cigarette. Our genes are as sensitive to any internal self-loathing as our feelings are to criticism from others. The best chance we have for getting past the traumatic experience of slavery is if we stop just saying, "We are Black and Proud" and begin to prove we are with the cessation of disfigering our skin and judging our beauty by European standards.

"Class and style has more to do with our character and attitude than the clothing we wear."

We can conclude that our genes will become supportive of our overall improved health and strength, when we wear our skin as a shield of honor as opposed to a badge of shame. We do not have to allow trauma to continue to rule and abide in our gene pool. The insanity can stop here with us and this generation, we have the means inherent in our ability to see the "Man and Woman in the Mirror as the fairest of them all."

Step 4
Acceptance of master's Standards

"A peoples' culture is composed of their beliefs, habits (traditions) and morals," Marty Hines (Knowledge Corner). To accomplish this portion of his methodology for the making of slaves, Willie Lynch, brought into play the oldest trick in the book when it comes to not only suppressing a people but also oppressing them. He let the white slave owners know that all they had to do was play the "Superior Culture Card." With this card they could seal the deal of keeping us in slavery for a thousand years, if not physically, at least psychologically and emotionally.

The "Superior Culture Card" is generally played in three ways;

1. It seeks to change the other person's personal beliefs about who he is in relation to civilization and the right to rule (Self-determination), This practice eventually became known as "Classical Conditioning, which Ivan Petrovich Pavlov, a Russian physiologist, was credited with demonstrating through his "Dog Experiment."

Classical conditioning (also known as Pavlovian or respondent conditioning) is a behavioral mechanism in which a biologically potent stimulus (e.g. food) is paired with a previously neutral stimulus (e.g. a bell). It also refers to the learning process that results from this pairing, through which the neutral stimulus comes to elicit a response (e.g. salivation) that is usually similar to the one elicited by the potent stimulus.

Classical conditioning is distinct from operant conditioning (also called instrumental conditioning), through which the strength of a voluntary behavior is modified by reinforcement or punishment. However, classical conditioning can affect operant conditioning in various ways; notably, classically conditioned stimuli may serve to reinforce operant responses.

I believe the way this was used in causing our ancestors to at least superficially accept white's standards, was rewarding them any time they showed a willingness to comply with whatever the master said was best for them, namely, in reference, to them doing what he demanded. When praise didn't work, there was always the whip to drive the message home, that "White was Right," therefore, it was wise for them to concede to the master's wishes, even if it was demeaning for them to do so, for the sake of saving their skin or wife, husband or child.

After slavery and Jim Crow was defeated, (albeit replaced with "The New Jim Crow.") and we were allowed to integrate into the mainstream white culture and society, the process of accepting white's standards continues. It is natural for us to assimilate if we want to advance as a race (Americans). We effectively cut off our nose to spite our face, in the sense that we have yet to recognize the conditioning that continues to drive us further and further from our own culture and norms.

In other words, "New Boss, Same Game!"

2. Getting the other person addicted to behaviors that are self-defeating, causing them tobecome habitual excuse makers (under-achievers). If I knock you down every time you stand up from the time you are a child until you become an adult, at some point, you will consider whether it is better to stop standing up and save yourself undue pain and suffering. Combine this with the fact that if I keep throwing it in your face that I am better than you, as evident by my superior living standards absent your ability to refute my claim, it becomes a foregone conclusion that you will suffer some damage to your sense of self-esteem.

It is human nature for us to draw our sense of self-worth as much from internal dignity as well as our social status, important to the development of our culture and/or society (family, community). What this did to our ancestors was cause them to snitch on each other to gain brownie points with the white master, resulting in a general distrust among the slaves themselves, any time the idea was suggested that they rebel. "Today snitches get dealt with!" So now we don't snitch on each other, even if it means continuing to have to live with runaway violence in our homes and neighborhoods.

3. Demoralizing the other person with the repeated accusation that he is a moraldegenerate as evidenced by his abject state of poverty and pervasive lack of cultural sophistication. In essence we were traumatized through the process of our culture along with our very selves being supplanted with the Proclamation that only that which was white could be deemed worth pursuing. As our ancestors were either forced or persuaded to acclimate to white culture (beliefs, habits, and morals) while being tortured if caught holding onto their own, they invariably felt a sense of belittlement that cut to their core.

We can perceive how this aspect of slavery could have had a devastating influence on our DNA, by taking note of our present habit of gravitating more toward white standards to this day. I cannot prove it, but I am, nevertheless, inclined to believe that a subtle dislike of self can be built up in an individual as well as an entire race, to the degree that it results in cellular degeneration. This seems not only possible to me but also probable based on the supposition that "As a man thinks in his heart, so is he." The heart being the soul of man, it doesn't take a genius to figure out that if it touches the soul, it touches every living cell within us.

The bottom line is that environmental stressors can alter cells on a monicula level and thus be passed through DNA to offspring. At some point the weaker and altered cell will become dominant and have a verified effect on the functioning of our overall physiology and innate behavior and responses to the environment that created such altered cells. (Wikipedia).

How we stop the transference of this genetic mutation to the next generation is by reasserting our cultural standards as Supreme and worthy of acceptance. I believe that the collective work we do to immerse ourselves in our culture (beliefs, habits, and morals) and the uplifting of each other, will prove a Game Changer as far as producing genes which transmit strength and not trauma – a sense of dignity, defined by self-reliance and self-determination.

Step 5
Deep Sense of Helplessness
and Dependence

Fear of the dark and imagining what could happen if you leave the safety of our front porch, works just as well as our captors having watch dogs to guard us. Once fear is instilled in a person or group the job of keeping them in line becomes significantly easier. That is why ghost stories work so well in scaring us, they play on our known fears. Willie Lynch understood the importance of creating a pervasive sense of helplessness in our ancestors as a means of assuring their complacency. In their case, their fear was not simply **FALSE EVIDENCE APPEARING REAL**, it was based on the daily cruelty of white slave masters toward any one of them who attempted to usurp their power over them. Until this day the vast majority of us still confuse our seemingly hopeless conditions with our being helpless.

Hope serves best those who know that they are never helpless, regardless of the odds against them. "The abyss of despair has no bottom as long as the abysmal has a hand to reach up with."

While we no longer fill the coffers of America's enterprises with the proceeds of our forced-free-labor, we now fill it with the wages we earn as wage-slaves instead of pouring the money into building up our own communities. Independence is achieved by becoming less dependent on others for the necessities of life. Even if we cannot physically separate from white society and the American political system, it is possible for us to regulate where our effort, time and money goes as far as building institutions that support True Liberation, beginning with a Liberation Education Curriculum for our children, which will produce entrepreneurs and not laborers.

Assimilation is unacceptable when separation is at least mentally feasible. The Bible encourages us to be in the world (America) but not of the world (America). We can do this by plotting a course that ultimately leads to the manifestation of "The strong men and women, who keep coming on, stronger and stronger," **STERLING BROWN. STRONG MEN**. 1931.

Our hope must not be rooted in God parting the Red Sea for us once again, but be based on our ability to shake the foundation of Heaven, losing it where it rains down new mercies. We can use God's favor to inspire us to take charge of our own fate, thus providing us with the confidence that we can overcome the trauma of slavery. It has been helpful that we have strived to "Keep Hope Alive" but I believe it would be good if we came to see our situation as being desperate to the point that we start to take revolutionary actions to improve it and ourselves. It can almost be said that we have been hopeful to a fault, in the sense that we have allowed our hope to surpass our resolve to, "Have Liberty or Death!" The hopeful farmer will wait until the cows come in before he closes the barn doors, where the desperate farmer will go out and get them, and thus close the barn doors when he is ready to do so.

"The reasonable man adapts himself to the world: the unreasonable one persists in trying to adapt the world to himself. Therefore all progress depends on the unreasonable man." — **George Bernard Shaw, Man and Superma**n.

Reason has always dictated that we 'wait' on better times and cooler heads, but it has never commanded an immediate and total removal of the status quo.

"For years now I have heard the word "Wait!" It rings in the ear of every Negro with piercing familiarity. This "Wait" has almost always meant "Never." We must come to see, with one of our distinguished jurists, that "justice **too long delayed is justice denied**,"" Dr. Martin Luther King, jr.

"Justice delayed is justice denied" is a legal maxim. It means that if legal redress or equitable relief to an injured party is available, but is not forthcoming in a timely fashion, it is effectively the same as having no remedy at all.

With it duly noted by Mr. Shaw and Dr. King, that there comes a time in every society and revolution when the waiting and hoping must end and action and determination must begin, it is obvious that both reason and hope, have expiration dates on their usefulness concerning the "changing of the tide and the guard." The transference of trauma through our DNA to our offspring ends now or never!

Hope outlives its usefulness any time it keeps us on our knees praying for a miracle of deliverance instead of causing us to stand on our feet and fight for freedom, as defined by the ability to conceive a dream, pursue a dream and achieve a dream (life) unmolested and unhindered by prejudice individuals and/or governmental institutions.

This bit of trickery creating "A deep sense of helplessness and dependenc" on Willie Lynch's behalf was his Opus Maximum, as far as traumatizing our ancestors to the extent that they allowed themselves to be subjected to the most dehumanizing, form of slavery in history for over three-hundred years. Exactly, "What was this master move and how has it haunted us to this day?" Before I offer an answer to this question, I first want to say that this is sadly the most debilitating genetic mutation that has been passed down through the generations of all those formerly enslaved.

Having said that, I will spell out how this trick was played on our ancestors and how it continues to be played on us today, where it perpetuates the very trauma we say we want to end. The "Art of War" prescribes that the most effective way to conquer and subject a people, is not what you would think, by saying their hope must be crushed. "Hope buried in the earth will eventually rise up again." If you really want to subdue a man or culture to the point that he will "Go to the back door without being told, and if there isn't one there for him, he will cut one out, so that he can enter in his accustomed manner,' (Carter G. Woodson, 'Miseducation of the Negro,' 1933), you simply have to breed into him a 'Deep sense of helplessness and dependence."

The evidence speaks for itself that whites succeeded in this final step to making us slaves. The proof is seen in how until this day we look to the very people who enslaved us to now give us the means to remove them from their seat of power – dominance. We sing it in church, "God bless the child who has his own," yet we still act like we can't help ourselves do what needs to be done in the achievement of True Liberation and Independence. When we have learned to become self-reliant and ask help from no other quarters, especially from those who have ever had our best interest at heart, we will invariably witness a healthy growth and improvement in our character, culture and ultimately in our DNA. Subsequently, we will no longer pass our trauma to our children nor replicate it in our "thinking, beliefs or behavior." Therefore, conceding that while we may be down, 'We are not helpless now, nor have we ever been," meaning, that we must shatter the chains of slavery and become independent.

Footnote:

Racism was not the reason why whites enslaved our ancestors nor is it the cause of our current impoverishment or trauma. Before we were found to be the perfect people for working in the cotton fields of the south, the settlers brought white prisoners over from England to pick cotton. After they were unsuccessful in using white prisoners, they experimented with white indentured servants. Who also proved unable to withstand the oppressive heat and toiling labor it took to plant and harvest cotton and other crops. Finally, they attempted to enslave Native Americans before finding us to be the only race that could do the work and who could not blend into the larger society as easily as indentured servants or into the wilderness like the Native Americans. "Slavery was all about money!"

Today racism is a continuation of the institutionalization of economic exploitation, which keeps the privileged, in a position of privilege, at the expense of our learned dysfunction. To redress the trauma of slavery, we must reprogram not only our thinking and behavior but also our genetics to generate optimistic cells, stoping the reproduction of pessimism in our metabolism.

It is not enough that we have been "set free" (those who are set free by man can be imprisoned and recaptured) from slavery through Abraham Lincoln"s, Act of Emancipation Proclamation (January 1, 1863). We must be "made free " (those who are made free by God are 'free indeed' never to be put in bondage again due to an inner-transformation of their mind, heart and soul. John 8:36 Kjv), carried over to the actualization of our highest concept of self-empowerment and what it means to be, "The sons and **daughters** of God for whom the whole of Creation is waiting on the manifestation of," (Romans 8:19 Kjv).

*P.S. "My past is an armour I cannot take off, no matter how many times you tell me the war is over." - **unknown.*** Our past as much shields us and traps us. At some point we have to dare to trade its protection for the freedom of living outside of it.

Appendix

Changing Lives and Communities Through the Improvement of Our Self-Image

Objective

To identify and redirect thoughts and behaviors that contribute to dysfunctional lives, families and communities.

Preface

My life changed forever in 2008, while in Elgin Mental Health Center, for the criminally insane. That was the time that I realized that if I wanted to change the road I had been on for thirty years of going in and out of prison, rehab and mental hospitals, I was going to have to change the picture I had of myself in my head. Up until that time I had seen myself as a three-time loser and drug addict, who had walked out on my wife and child, thus that is the image I conformed to for the majority of my life. The miracle came when I decided that I would no longer picture myself as a criminal and loser but would start to see myself as a writer, public speaker and winner.

Since I changed the mental image I had of myself thirteen years ago, I have been able to live the life of my dream, breaking the vicious cycle of failure and disappointment that had previously entrapped me. Therefore, you can believe me when I tell you, "The picture you have of yourself in your head, is the image you will conform to." To get a better life, draw a better self-image of yourself in your head. That is the purpose of this book, to help you improve your self-image, therefore, changing your life and how you influence your family and community.

Introduction

The problems of crime, violence, addiction, poverty, suicide and broken homes are all symptoms of the real problem in the African American community, which is, OUR POOR SELF-IMAGE. Why do we have a poor self-image? I believe it is because we have accepted white people's interpretation and telling of our history, that we are on a rise up from slavery instead of descendants of greatness. We are already behind the Eightball when we start our story from the point we were kidnapped from our home (AFRICA) and brought to America, to be beaten, raped and belittled for four-hundred years. Thus, we are obviously in desperate need of a total Makeover of Our Self-Image.

Seeing ourselves as coming from a place and position of degradation, we subject ourselves to all forms of defacement and belittlement. If our poor self-image is causing us to go in the direction of those who are on their way out as opposed to that of those on their way in, it is obvious that we need to change our image. "Where there is no vision the people perish," (Proverbs 29:18). What vision do we have for ourselves and of ourselves? What is the meaning of "self-image?"

"Our self-image is what we think about ourselves," Joshua Coakley. A more vivid definition of self-image says, "The picture we have of ourselves in our head (mind) is the image we will conform to," Danny Christian. The greatest work we need to do in our community is improve the image we have of ourselves. This makeover program is created to do just that.

Overview

Generally, our family, more specifically, our parent's history and legacy is the baseline at which we start in building our own legacy and forming our self-image.

Before a new image can be shaped, the old mold must be broken. In other words, if we have been taught and told that, "We are the descendants of slaves and our history did not begin until Europeans discovered us living on a "Dark Continent," we are less likely to feel as proud of ourselves as we would if the truth was told, and it noted that we are in fact "The First Man of Creation" and "God's Chosen People."

Therefore, let us not start the conversation by talking about Booker T. Washington's Autobiography, "Up From Slavery," as though that was our greatest accomplishment. Before we can begin the process of reshaping our self-image, it is important that we ascertain in whose "Image" we are made as well as from what "Culture" we were cast. For too long have we allowed slavery to cast a dark and discouraging shadow over us here in America. The time and day has come where it is now a matter of life or death, that we cast a "New Shadow " over the world in which we live and have been mocked as though we; come from nothing, have nothing and are nothing.

There have been countless television shows where people have been given cosmetic makeovers, which transformed their lives, and gave them a whole new sense of self-confidence. For this reason seeing how a simple cosmetic makeover can change an individual's life and sense of confidence, I am confident that the same thing can happen for a family, community and race that reshapes its self-image – Give Itself a Makeover.

The start of a new history, starts with a new self-image; which requires some simple changes to three aspects of our character and behavior. Most notably, changing how we, Think, Feel and Talk. When we make adjustments to these three areas, we see a significant improvement not only in how we feel about ourselves, but also in how we respond and interact with each other. It is no small matter that we pay close attention to the "thoughts we think, the feelings we feel and the words we speak." Based on the quality and focus of our thoughts, feelings and conversation, we will be judged as either deserving of room at the decision table or a table in the kitchen with the servants.

Enough said, let us take a look at how we can redress the negative issues caused by our current poor self-image through the reshaping of our personal self-images.

3 Steps to change your thinking:

Thoughts (Your Perspective) determine your reality
(As a man thinketh in his heart, so is he. Proverbs 23:7 kjv)

Because "We feel like we think and act like we feel," it is important at the start that we understand the first step to improving our self-image as individuals who form a family, community and race, is to examine our thought processes, to determine if they are hurting us or helping us. The remedy to feeling poor and/or unworthy is to stop thinking such thoughts about ourselves. "We are conscious beings, who manifest thoughts, which translate into feelings, resulting in matching actions."

1. **Rethink the questions you ask**

"Judge a man by his questions rather than his answers," Voltaire. Nothing is accomplished by us continuing to ask the obvious questions as to why this or that has befallen us as individuals, a family, community and race? I am confident that we will become prouder of ourselves when we ask more probing questions of ourselves as to why we have left it to others, to elevate their thinking to the Tenth-Power? The bottom line is that our minds cannot provide us with any answers we do not ask for. Let us cease to ask "why" and begin to ask "Why not?' Why not questions tend to be more challenging and inspiring than why questions. In the end that is really what we want to know, "Why can't we be the people who end world hunger, bring about world peace and cure all illnesses?"

(Improve imagination)

"There is nothing that is real which wasn't first imagined, nor is there anything impossible which can be imagined." We need to know that our lives are only limited by the scope of our imagination. If we put no limits on it (GOD), it (HE) won't put any limits on us.

To live the unimagined life, we must first imagine it, once that is done, it is just a matter of time before we are experiencing the life of our dreams.

How we improve our imagination:

Look for what is present, see the glass as half-full. Only what we see with our mind's eye, can we hold in our hands or experience. A major key to developing an improved self-image is seeing ourselves in light of who we say we are and who God says we are, "A chosen nation and royal priesthood, a peculiar people," and not as society portrays us or our past shadows us.

I have personally experienced greater success by asking "How can I do something" instead of asking "Why things happened the way they did in the past?" Asking how has helped me stay focused on the present and looking forward, where when I asked why, I wasted valuable time and energy focusing on the past. Therefore, to improve our self-image it is advised that we spend more time and energy looking for ways to build up ourselves and our community.

2. Rethink the answers you consider

If we are honest with ourselves, we would admit that a lot of times we already have the answers we are going to consider and settle for before we ask the question. Speaking for myself when I do this, it is because I know that if I remain open minded and allow God to speak to me, that either He or my best mind may give me an answer that I am uncomfortable with, and will require me doing what is right as opposed to doing what is convenient.

We are prejudiced by our past as to what answers we are going to consider if it means that we are going to have to admit our own complicity in creating our problems. When we are ready to rethink the answers to our most pressing questions (challenges) I believe that we will start to see ourselves in a brighter light, which shows our ingenuity.

How we improve our optimism:

Be students of our mistakes. As opposed to looking at our mistakes as a sign of failure, we should look at them as proof that we have dared to step out on faith, and try to do things different from the status quo. I am certain that our mistakes will serve us better if we use them to grow instead of as dirt to bury us. When we take ownership of our mistakes we also take responsibility for our success. "We never have to be ashamed of anything that has enriched our spirit (culture), expanded our mind (imagination) or strengthened our faith (confidence)." We can each become the picture of optimism by simply embracing our reputation for being **"BRAGGADOCIOS and AUDACIOUS!!!"**

3. Rethink the decisions you make

It has been said that "first we make our choices then our choices make us." With this thought in mind, I want to make it clear to everyone seeking to improve their self-image, and thereby their life opportunities as well as effectiveness, that if we do not take control of our thoughts and emotions, we will not control anything else. "A wise man takes his time in making his decisions but once they are made, he acts swiftly." It says a lot about us when people see us strategically plotting our course and sticking to it through thick and thin. Even if we do not have all the answers it is still recommended that we act with decisiveness, using the information and resources we do have. It has been my experience that when I just go with what I know and am capable of that "The teacher appears" with the tools I need to carry the lesson further, to its conclusion.

How we improve our decisiveness:

Let the buck start and stop with us. Becoming resolute is one of the best ways I know to help in building self-confidence which in-turn improves one's self-image. Therefore, try to make it a habit from this day forward to stick to the plans and commitments you have made to; 1. be a doer and 2. be true to thyself. Make it your business to think it through and then follow through as a means of proving yourself to be reliable and thorough.

New thought you want to embrace:______________________________

Once you have chosen the new thought you want to embrace, let it germinate in your mind until you have decided how you are going to use it as a means of taking your life in a new direction, which reflects your improved self-image.

Results:

Our mind will produce a better mental self-image by changing what we think about ourselves.

Improving our self-image is not a one time and one-day event, it is on-going and requires continual adaptation to this makeover program. For that reason, you want to embrace a new thought/idea every day as a means of acquiring new wisdom, knowledge and insight.

3 Steps to change your feelings:

Feelings drive your actions.

Feelings are the fruit of our thoughts and attitude; to control and master them we must watch our thoughts. Some of us are more emotional than others, and have a reputation for acting out our feelings before we have filtered them. In order to further improve our self-image, it is necessary that we work on building our Emotional Intelligence (EQ). Psychologists are starting to learn and believe that Emotional Intelligence is just as important as our Mental Intelligence (IQ). If our self-image has been less than we desire it to be because of our past mishandling of certain situations because we allowed our emotions to take control, now is the time for us to look at the source of such emotions.

1. **Exchange feeling of distrustfulness for benefits of vulnerability**

It is a big plus to our self-image when people know that we are not afraid to feel and express the whole gambit of our emotional spectrum. Our emotional courage shows through our ability and willingness to be vulnerable. In other words, we want to overcome being so defensive when it comes to letting others either get close to us or making emotional investments in others. Our emotional courage and strength shows in the way we carry ourselves around those who attempt to manipulate our emotions. While we may be "suckers for love" we are not "emotional crash dummies." That is, we know where and when to be vulnerable and transparent, and when and where to set boundaries.

How we create room for change:

A change in how we act is preceded by a change in how we feel. "Our actions (the sum total of our lives) are the chick that hatches from the egg of our emotions." There is a time for us to sit on our emotions, allowing them to incubate, and a time to hatch them as they come to maturity. Because our feelings are as much a part of our character as our thoughts and actions, we should do all we can to know where they come from, and why we either hold on to them too long, or constantly air and relive them.

Value risk and the benefit of opening yourself up to others.

Improving our self-image involves improving the quality of our relationships and the type of people we associate with. If you already have a bad attitude, you do not want to be around others who are only going to add more fuel to any explosive emotions you have. "Beware of Emotional Poison," which is the product of distrust and resentment. As we attempt to improve our self-image it is essential that we accept that while all emotions are valid, all emotions are not healthy. The way we find out which ones are healthy and which are unhealthy, is by asking ourselves, "Do they validate us or condemn us?" Thus, we want to keep those which validate us and weed out all those that condemn us. When we do this we will witness a noted improvement in the way we feel about ourselves and all those we interact with on an emotional level. **(Avoid feelings of victimization but allow feelings of victory)**

"Feelings of victimization are the deadliest!" Regardless of what others may have done to you or how many struggles you have, calling yourself a 'victim' is the least effective way to become self-empowered. After discarding 'Stinking thinking' you want to discard 'Feelings of Victimization,' as a prerequisite to improving your self-image. Know that if you are still here in any condition after the pain, you are a "VICTOR' not a victim. Victims do not live to tell their story because either they did not survive the attack on their life or they have given up on themselves. Whatever has happened to you, no one can make you a victim, that is your choice to make or identity to take on, according to your desire to live in the past or move on. The minute others agree with your conclusion that you are a victim, know that they are not looking at your strength that got you through, but the weakness and defeat you claim.

2. **Exchange feelings of secretiveness for benefits of transparency**

"We Wear the Mask," (Paul Laurence Dunbar), needlessly. The best us live behind the mask we wear to keep our secrets hidden. Yet, the reality is that our secrets always seep through the cracks in our mask (the facade we put on to make others think we are "All Well"). To improve our image it is important that we disarm our secrets, meaning that we come out of the closet about whatever makes us ashamed of being our true-selves. "Transparency looks better on us than any mask." Being transparent simply means that you are honest with yourself and others about how you feel and why you feel the way you do about any particular person or situation (experience).

How we create greater openness:

"It is better to be an open book than a closed tomb," for the simple reason that as open books we give a clearer expression and representation of our FAITH, HOPE and EXPERIENCES, which contribute to our overall character and legacy. In pursuit of an improved self-image it is helpful that we open up more about our expectations of ourselves, others and the society in which we live. Put another way, I would say that we should expose our true feelings and intentions before they expose us. Being open enables us to pour good things out of our treasure of wisdom and faith into others as well as allow others to share their gifts with us. In the end everybody wins when we come clean about who we are, what we are, where we come from and where we are heading.

3. **Exchange feelings of selfishness for benefits of accountability**

Altruism and accountability are two valuable characteristics we want to add to our character resume as we move forward in continuing to improve our self-image. Hopefully we will get to the point where we will feel obligated to be accountable to all those who depend on us and have confidence in us, and where they will feel free to call on us for assistance any time they are in need. Up until this point we have been known to be more concerned about our own welfare without caring about the general wellbeing of our "Village." When it is every man for himself, nobody wins, and the individual misses the chance to add their mix to the "Kool Aid" we make better together.

How we create greater integrity:

Once we lose the respect and trust of others it is hard to regain it but not impossible. When repairing or trying to improve our reputation and/or self-image it is important that we begin by keeping our promise, or better yet, that we simply say what we are going to do and do it without taking any vows. Integrity is a significant component of good character, it is built slowly and torn down quickly when we lie, steal or cheat. Therefore, if we are to succeed at improving our self-image it is imperative that we not take people's trust in us for granted. The greatest compliment someone can give us is to say that we are men and women of "integrity." Thus, we should work to achieve it as though it were the most precious diamond, and hold tight to it once we have it.

Allow others to hold you to your word.

It helps our self-image in a big way when the people in our lives know that if we tell them that we are to do something that they can count on us doing it to the letter. Each time we follow through on our plans and promises it is another feather in our cap as far as improving our self-image. The trade for us, allowing others to hold us to our word, is that we can hold others to their word. It's an equal exchange; accountability for accountability.

(Avoid feelings of separateness but allow feelings of connection)

The basic reason we want to connect with our peers (tribe) is because we naturally feel better and do better when there are other people around us with the same mindset and objectives. "We are generally only as healthy and positive as the people we associate with the most." Each day it helps in the improvement of our self-image when we build stronger connections with God, family and community. I believe that our self-image improves to the degree that we reach out to others with our hearts' request to be embraced simply because it is there – open and welcoming to all hugs and kisses.

New feeling you want to experience _______________________________

Once you have chosen the new feeling you want to experience, note why it is important that you add it to your emotional reservoir, as a means of improving your (EQ), which will in-turn improve your self-image.

Results:

Our heart will produce a better emotional self-image by changing our level of confidence. 3 Steps to change your talk:

Words express your attitude

"Our attitude and conversation are reciprocal," one can be no more positive or negative than the other. Both our self-image and reputation suffers to the extent that we let negative and self-defeating or demoralizing words come out of our mouth. It is absolutely imperative that we make a positive change in the way we talk before we can start to see an improvement in our self-image. The words we speak and how we express them speak for the type of people we are and how we feel about ourselves. To repair any damage that has been done to our self-image by our past mistakes, we must enamor ourselves with words of "Self-praise and Affirmation." What we say about ourselves is more important to building our self-image than what anyone else says about us – the way we used to be.

1.   Reshape words of hopelessness to words of hopefulness

"Death and life are in the power of the tongue: and they that love it shall eat the fruit thereof," Proverbs 18:21 kjv. Life or death will follow and be produced by every word we speak and every thought we think before speaking. Hopeless thoughts and words will create hopeless feelings just as hopeful thoughts and words will create feelings of hope. Even if our situation is so trying that we cannot help feeling hopeless, we must know that we are never "helpless." We have to assure ourselves that as long as we can fight back, we can come back. The foundation of the improved self-image we are trying to build is established on the conversation we have with ourselves in our heads. Just as when building a new house, you have to demolish the old structure, you have to demolish your old self-talk before you can start a new life and image.

How we increase our sense of usefulness:

A simple fact of life and psychology is that the more useful we feel to others, the better we feel about ourselves. "Our self-esteem grows out of the esteemable things we do," Billy brown. Conversely, the more esteemable things we do, the higher our self-esteem will be. The key to increasing our sense of usefulness is that it is for us to say and prove how useful we are.

An applicable cliché here is, "One man's junk is another man's treasure." In other words we need to know that just because others may deem us useless or used-up, that we can still have value and use to ourselves and a different set of people in a different set of circumstances. Therefore, we want to affirm our usefulness by letting our conversation be as loving and positive as possible. We have the power to influence how society sees us and how we see ourselves by generating progressive dialogue among people who are committed to building a better society and opportunities for all.

(Speak courageously not disparagingly)

How and what we think and say about others reflects who we are more than it reflects them. Put simply, we cannot be thinking or talking bad about others and feel good about ourselves at the same time. (It is a bad habit to put others down in an attempt to build ourselves up). One of the easiest things we can do to improve our self-image is to begin praising others as much as we affirm our own "GREATNESS!!!" As we find more ways to build others up through sincere praise and encouragement, we will create better feelings about ourselves. The reality is that we cannot build others up without at the same time building ourselves up; just as we tire ourselves down when we put others down. "Criticism corrodes the character of the cynic more than it does those who are criticized." It takes but a little change in the way we talk about ourselves as well as others to achieve significant improvements in our self-image.

2. Reshape words of hurt/pain to words of healing/kindness

"When we look in the mirror, do we see the rawness of our wound and pain or the pink scab of our healing and victory?" We do the most to improve our self-image by what we call our wound (past), noting that we make it whatever we name it. We must realize that we always have the option of letting our past be a weight around our neck pulling us down or wind at our back propelling us forward. After Saul's Damascus Road encounter with Jesus, where he was asked, "**3** As he journeyed he came near Damascus, and suddenly a light shone around him from heaven. **4**

Then he fell to the ground, and heard a voice saying to him, "Saul, Saul, why are you persecuting Me?" **Acts 9 (NKJV)**, his name was changed from Saul to Paul. The point is that once we have been truly transformed by any life experience, a change in name must accompany the transformation, to signify that we are no longer the people we used to be. In short, if the old us were people who wore their wound and pain on their sleeve, the new us must now wear it as a shield that saved us. Despite all the good that Saul thought he was doing by breathing words of hatred for the Christians, Jesus made him realize that he was actually persecuting the very God he called himself protecting. We in the same sense sometimes have to be shaken to our core in order to be put back on track.

How we increase our sense of compassion:

We can blame past abuse and betrayal of our trust and love for causing us to harden our heart, but it is our responsibility to return them to flesh. The only way we do this, as a further step to improving our self-image, is to let feelings of compassion return to our heart and soul. To increase our sense of compassion all we have to do is become passionate about life once again. Our compassion flows from our "Passion." Our passion and the compassion it generates will brighten our demeanor, leading to an elevation of our self-image. We heighten our interest in life by the things we are passionate about which causes us to display greater compassion towards both others and ourselves.

Talk to others as you want to be talked to and with the same honesty.

We have all been told since childhood that, "If it is good for the goose, it's good for the gender." This is a cute way of letting us know that we should not do nor say anything to others that we do not want them to do or say to us. It always helps improve the way we feel and talk about ourselves and the importance of our lives (gifts) when we have a job. One way we can improve our self-image is by becoming a voice for the voiceless. As a means of making amends for our past misdeeds we can do our reputation a lot of good by making it our mission to speak words of truth and convey wholesome ideas when we talk to others.

3. Reshape words of negativity to words of positivity

"A word fitly spoken is like apples of gold in pictures of silver," Proverbs 25:11 (KJV). The right word or comment at the right time can change the whole trajectory of someone's life as well as their self-image. We can concurrently improve our own self-image as we help others feel better about themselves through the things we say to them and about them. Negative words should be used sparingly, if at all, while positive words should be used liberally and frequently. As we incorporate more uplifting words into our vocabulary, we will do a great service to the enhancement of self-image. Knowing this, there is never a good way to criticize someone, no more than there is a bad way to pay someone a compliment. Therefore, we should not attempt to do the former, where we can always find occasion to do the latter.

How we increase our sense of opportunity:

In one way or another every word we have uttered and prayed up until this moment has led to us being where we are right now. "In the beginning was the Word and the Word was with God, and the Word was God (Supreme) by him nothing was made, that is made," Genesis 1:1 (KJV). Since the beginning of time, words, which are thoughts made manifest, (thoughts become words and words become things – our reality) have had creative powers. "They bear fruit" or in other words, have consequences. The point is that we can add to our self-image in a positive way by tailoring our conversation to reflect the new opportunities we want to experience. If the old you was known for pointing out the emptiness of the glass, let the new you describe how the glass is half-full. With the words of our mouth we have the power and means to radically transform not only our own lives but the world in which we live. "Our words say who we are and who we are adds power to them – our WORDS!!!"

(Speak with purpose or be quiet until you have something meaningful to say)

Finally, we can improve our self-image by spending time in meditation and reflection so that when we open our mouths to speak, our words will bear being heard and contemplated by our audience. The sophistication of our ideas and words says the most about the caliber of our character and the magnitude of our intellect, therefore, we should do all that we can to learn as many powerful and inspiring words as possible. We call the letters of the alphabet, "Characters," because each one of them has their own intonation (meaning that they conjure up certain spirits and images), history and manner of expression. Likewise, our words are symbols of our character which prescribe how we are to be addressed and noticed. The crowning touch on the creation of our New and Improved Self-Image is made with a new way of not only talking the talk but walking the walk. "We can do this, be all that 'The Creator' made us to be; BOLD BEAUTIFUL AND MASTERFUL!!

New word you want to use: ________________________________

Once you have found a new word you want to add to your vocabulary, research its history and root meaning, and then attempt to use it as much as possible in your general conversations, so that it can help improve your self-image by building your vocabulary and communication skills.

Results:
Our better talk will strengthen our relationships by empowering us to be PROACTIVE and PROUD.

I Am
"Anything you say after, I Am, the mind will believe and the universe will agree with, bringing it to reality."

9 781664 109629